Paris Terrorist Attack

Why the Terrorists Terrorized Charlie Hebdo Magazine

Burning Reports
Topics, Issues, Current Events & More

Disclaimer

Summary

The attack on the Charlie Hebdo offices in Paris shocked the world with many governments coming out strongly to condemn it. There are many people who did not know the events that led to this attack and what followed.

This *Burning Report* contains information that explains the reasons that could have led to the Paris shooting, what happened during the attack and the subsequent attacks, the reaction of the citizens of France and the world at large, the steps taken to bring the perpetrators to justice, the population of Muslims in France and Europe, how Muslims are viewed in these areas, if there were any clues that the police and government could have used to prevent the attack, other attacks that have happened in France and on the Charlie Hebdo news magazine in the previous years and how the people of France treated the attack.

This *Burning Report* will enlighten you on the Paris shooting and the war against terror in Europe and you will be in a position to understand what happened and the reasons behind them.

Table of Contents

Introduction

Charlie Hebdo the satire magazine in France had made a great impact in the country, though they were not known by many outside France until the 7th of January 2015. They made news worldwide when they were attacked by terrorists over some cartoons they had been publishing about Mohammed and about Islam. Although they had previously received threats over their actions, they never stopped.

This French satirical news magazine has been around for a period of forty-four years and in most of those years it has used humor to express itself. The magazine has published many cartoons over the years that contain the images of Prophet Muhammad. This is considered as blasphemy in Islam and it is punishable by death.

The Cartoons that Angered the Charlie Hebdo News Magazine Attackers

Charlie Hebdo has been known to openly ridicule Prophet Muhammad and the obsession of some of his followers. Due to their refusal to cower before Islam and the religious icon whose beliefs they do not share, they have been targeted by many extremists and have faced constant threats of violence. Despite all of this, they continued to satirize Islam. However, they did this for other religions as well and not just Islam. They stood out in France because they tackled a topic about which most people were afraid of discussing.

Twelve people would later pay for the freedom of expression that the Charlie Hebdo magazine had been exercising when their offices were attacked. The French President Francois Hollande gave a statement after the attack and described it as "a terrorist attack without a doubt". He later went on to say that France had faced several other attacks which they had been able to avert.

The satirical news magazine Charlie Hebdo had posted one of their cartoons of Abu Bakr al- Baghdadi on their twitter account. In the cartoon, the Islamic State Group's leader was being offered New Year's wishes by his staff. The Muslim extremists had demanded that Charlie Hebdo stop publishing the images of Prophet Muhammad but the news magazine continued doing so. The extremists were arguing that even the people who don't share their faith should submit to it.

There are a number of cartoons that the Charlie Hebdo had published that had offended the Muslim extremists. There was one published on October 2014 which had an ISIS fighter beheading Prophet Muhammad while the prophet was shouting, "I'm the prophet, you asshole and the killer responded by saying, "shut your trap, infidel."

There was a cartoon released in 2011 which had Muhammad acting as the editor- in- chief of the Charlie Hebdo magazine telling people that they will get one-hundred lashes in case that they do not die of laughter after reading the news magazine. The news magazine's offices were later firebombed due to this publication some weeks later. Fortunately no one was hurt during the attack.

There was a movie that Charlie Hebdo published titled, "The Innocence of Muslims" which talked about the U.S Embassy's attack in Benghazi. When Muslims reacted to this movie, Charlie Hebdo published a cartoon in which Muhammad was posing for a camera. It had a caption one side that read, "A star is born" and "The film that will set the Muslim world on fire" on the other side. There was a part where Muhammad was asking, "My ass? You love my ass?" There was another cartoon that followed saying that love is stronger than hate. This cartoon had Muhammad and Charlie Hebdo locking lips.

The government of France (in this case) defended the magazine saying it had a right to publish the cartoons. It went ahead to criticize the violent reaction that the cartoons had elicited. After the cartoons were published, the riot police camped outside of the magazine's offices to offer protection.

Another one of the popular Charlie Hebdo cartoons was their versions of the French film known as the "Untouchables". This film revolves around a rich white man who hires the services of a poor black man in taking care of him after being paralyzed in an accident. In the cartoon, the rich man was telling the poor man that he should not laugh.

As this was going on, French establishments expressed concern about this which prompted the police to request Stephane Charbonnier popularly known as Charb (who was the chief editor of the magazine) to reconsider their decision of publishing the issue. The news magazine went ahead and did it a week later. Immediately after publishing it, the French government tightened security and talked of closing around twenty foreign outposts. The French politicians condemned the cartoons and said they were irresponsible. The Prime Minister also criticized this move in his statement.

Charb has said in an earlier interview that Muhammad is not sacred to him and he understands why the Muslims do not find their cartoons hilarious. However, he went on to say that he lives under the French law and not the Quranic law. He was later to be among the twelve killed on the 7th Jan 2015. Tignous, Wolinski and Cabu are the other famous cartoonists in France who also died during the attack.

Jyllands-Posten, a Danish newspaper published images of Muhammad in 2006 which led to an outrage across the Islamic world and Charlie Hebdo took it from there and republished the images on the front cover of their issue. In the cartoon, Muhammad was complaining saying, "It's difficult to be loved by these idiots."

Muslim associations filed a complaint against Charlie Hebdo, but the news magazine was later acquitted in 2008 by the Paris appeal court. After the attack on the Charlie Hebdo news magazine building, Jyllands-Posten posted on their website that they had tightened their security bearing in mind that they had also published the images of Muhammad originally. Their staff was informed of the unspecified security measures via mail.

On the fateful day, gunmen got in to the Charlie Hebdo offices in Paris and opened fire while shouting, Allah hu –Akbar. They killed twelve people. Among those killed were two police officers who got in their way.

Some of Charlie Hebdo's famous cartoonists who were in charge of drawing the images of Muhammad were among the people that were killed. One of their cartoonists interviewed in the past had defended the drawings saying they were not provocations but merely cartoons.

There is a novel titled "Suomission" which means submission written by Michel Houellebecq. It revolves around an Islamic government being formed from 2022. It speaks of the French elections preferring a Muslim brotherhood-styled party instead of the traditional parties.

The book talks about a France with a Muslim president who establishes the Sharia Law. The women are forced to wear veils and stop working. The Sorbonne University in the book is renamed as the Paris-Sorbonne Islamic University. The book also has increased fears among the Europeans that their cultures are being attacked especially with a great number of Muslim immigrants coming to Europe to escape conflicts in Sudan, Syria and other countries. This has led to more strict anti-immigrant parties. Houellebecq, on the other hand, defends his book saying it is merely a political fiction although it can result in more resistance against Muslim immigration in Europe.

The latest issue of Charlie Hebdo News magazine has the cartoon of Michel Houellebecq's imaginations of France being under the Islamic rule. He is smoking a cigarette in the picture and says, "in 2015 I will lose my teeth" and then "in 2022 I will do Ramadan"

Muslims' Population in France and Europe

The Paris terrorist attacks followed by the protest marches in Germany have now brought up a question of the Muslim's position in a French society and their population in Europe.

There have been growing concerns in many European countries. Among those concerned are the United Kingdom, Germany and Netherlands with growing Muslim communities. This has led to even immigration or calls for restrictions. It makes one wonder how large the Muslim population is in Europe and the rate at which it is growing.

Although the government of France does not allow collecting of official statistics on the religion or race of its people, the population is estimated to be at around six million as at 2013. This information comes from several recent studies conducted in the attempt to find out the number of people who originated from Muslim majority countries. Of that population, five million are Muslims. This means that the population of France is about 10% of the total population of the country which is at 66 million people. France, therefore, has the largest number of Muslims in the European Union.

Half of the Muslim population in France is believed to be under the age of twenty-four. It is difficult to find concrete data, thus, these are just estimations due to the fact that the French Republic treats this as a private matter.

Marseille was declared to be the most dangerous city in all of Europe. Of its total population, thirty to forty percent is estimated to be Muslims. The city is greatly known for drug smuggling and has become a place where the police do not have control and gangsters rule. They import and sell the North African Hashish and arms are used to settle disputes.

In the previous years, the city had been given the honor of being "cultural capital of Europe". This distinction led to the creation of new tourist attraction ads launching of beautification projects. These ads attracted people from all over the world. There was even an amazing high-tech historical museum that was put up next to city hall and a stone esplanade around the old port. However, the positive results expected turned negative.

Studies conducted in 2010 showed that Germany and France lead with the largest number of Muslims in the European Union and the figures stood at 4.8 million making up 5.8% of the country's total population and 4.7 million making up 7.5 of the country's total population for Germany and France respectively. However, in Europe, Russia leads overall with the largest population of Muslims on the continent. It comes in at fourteen million, therefore occupying ten percent.

The Muslim population in Europe has grown over the decades with about one percent per decade rising from four percent to six percent between 1990 and 2010. If this pattern continues up to 2030, then the Muslims will make up to eight percent of the total population of Europe.

It has been discovered that the Muslims are younger compared to other Europeans. For example, Muslims had a median age of 32 in 2010 while all Europeans had a median age of forty. The median age of agnostics, atheists and those not affiliated by any religion in Europe was thirty-seven while those affiliated with Christianity was forty-two.

There are different views of Muslims across the European continent. Studies were conducted by the Pew Research Centre in 2014 to find out how Muslims were viewed in Europe and these were the results.

Unfavorable	**Muslims**	Favorable
26%	Britain	64%
27	France	72
33	Germany	58
53	Greece	43
63	Italy	28
50	Poland	32
46	Spain	49

France, Britain and Germany led with the highest number of people having a favorable view of Muslims. Spain had divided opinions while Italy, Greece and Poland had negative views of Muslims. The different ideologies that people have concerning Muslims are what influence their opinion of them. For example, 58% of Germans interviewed had a positive view about Muslims while 33% have a negative opinion of them. This goes to show that there is a gap in between the two groups of people may be who are not sure or whose views can change depending on their ideologies. The gap is also experienced in Italy, France and Greece.

The first Muslims migrated to France many centuries ago, although most of them moved in the contemporary era during the wars of independence that took place between 1954 and 1962. Marseille, Lyon and Paris, and their suburbs, are some of the major Muslim population centers.

The number of Muslim immigrants in the European Union was at thirteen million in 2010. Most of the foreign-born Muslims in Germany are of Turkish origin, although there are also others from Iraq, Morocco, Kosovo and Bosnia-Herzegovina. The estimated three million Muslims born in France originated from different countries, although a good number of them came from North Africa and mainly Morocco, Algeria and Tunisia, to be precise.

What Transpired on the Day of the Charlie Hebdo Attack?

Although Charlie Hebdo had faced threats before, due to their controversial publishing of the Prophet Muhammad and other religious leaders, they were not expecting the attack that took place on that fateful day.

One witness recalled seeing some people filming on the roof of the building while a Citroen C3 new car drove to the building and two guys emerged with black masks and fired at an unknown target using a Kalashnikov. One online video showed masked gunmen emerging from a black car before firing several shots and then firing at a policeman. The wounded policeman then raises his hands and asks for mercy before the gunmen shot him at point black range in the head. Afterwards, the gunmen drove away in their car. Another policeman was killed while trying to protect the Chief Editor, Stephane Charbonnier.

A source close to the investigation recalls seeing two men storming in to the Charlie Hebdo building while armed with a rocket –

launcher and Kalashnikov. Armed with these weapons, they exchanged fire with the security forces. The same source goes on to add that the gunmen hijacked a car and knocked down a pedestrian while speeding away.

A journalist working opposite the area used the words, "…pools of blood, bodies on the floor and some very serious injuries" to describe the scene he saw at the Charlie Hebdo offices. She went on to say that some people from the Charlie Hebdo building went to sit in their building to try and calm down after the attack was over.

Television footage shows multiple police officers within the vicinity of the building and bullet-riddled windows.

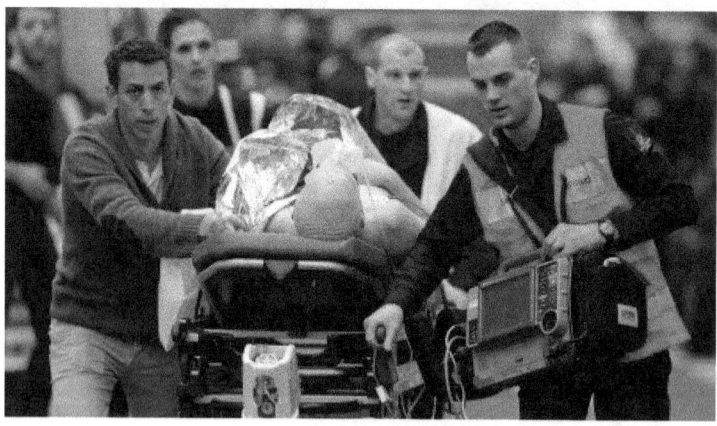

Some people were seen carried away on stretchers

A man who was taking refuge on a roof managed to take a video of the attack which he circulated online. In the video, there is a distinct sound of a man shouting while firing gun shots, "Allahu akbar" meaning "God is great". According to police sources, the gunmen were also shouting, "We have avenged the prophet".

A postal worker who witnessed the ordeal said that she was making a delivery when the attack started. She was inside the building, towards the end of the corridor, when some people came in looking for Charlie Hebdo. They proceeded to fire guns in order to scare the woman and those that accompanied her.

Bruno Leveille, a resident near the building heard gunshots at exactly 11:30 a.m. He estimated around thirty gunshots which were fired during the course of approximately ten minutes.

Minutes after the attack, it became breaking news with the various television channels showing live what was happening on the scene. The French officials set their national security alert system to, "attack alert" after the attack. This is considered to be the highest form of alert.

The attack on the satirical news magazine, Charlie Hebdo, left at least twelve fatalities is considered the deadliest attack that France has seen in forty years. The French minister referenced the attack when he tweeted that there were more tears than words which affected the employees and police of Charlie Hebdo and their families in general.

Reaction of Leaders Around the World

The Paris shooting was condemned worldwide with different governments offering their condolences and support in the fight against terror. David Cameron, the British Prime Minister, sent a tweet saying that he supports freedom of speech. He later went on to say that the French people have his support in the fight against terror. The gunmen claimed to be from the terrorist group, al-Qaeda.

The US President Barack Obama spoke in condemnation of the act and pledged assistance to the French people with regard to bringing the terrorists to justice. He went on to say that the United State would stand with them every day in the fight against terror. His exact words were, "We stand for freedom and hope and dignity of all human beings, that's what Paris stands for."

The FBI, together with the U.S. Department of homeland security, gave law enforcement forces across the entire United States a bulletin discussing the Paris terrorist attack that took place on the week of January 7th, 2015. It entailed the tactics that the terrorists employed and their level of sophistication. According to the bulletin the attacks had, "a degree of sophistication and training traditionally not seen in recent small armed attacks" said the official who read it.

Omer Celik, the Turkish minister in charge of culture and tourism, said that the Paris will heighten the already existing religious tensions in Europe. He went on to say that he could not defend Islam in the face of such a massacre.

Speaking on MSNBC, Josh Earnest the White House spokesman strongly condemned the shooting attack and said that the people at the White House sent their heartfelt condolences to the affected people.

President Vladimir of Russia sent his condolences to the bereaved families and strongly condemned all manner of terrorism. The same sentiments were echoed by Putin's spokesman Dmitry Peskov concerning Moscow's stand on terrorism. He further stated that there can never be justification for terrorist attacks. His condolences were sent to the people who lost their loved ones, those who were injured in the attack and to the French in general.

President Hollande of France gave a statement to the effect that the gunmen will be hunted down (no matter how long it takes), arrested and charged before the courts.

Stephen Harper, the Canadian Prime Minister, offered a statement the day following the attack. He stated that this attack confirmed that jihadists have declared war on the people who do not agree with them and conform to their way of thinking. He went on to say that we have to deal with the problem of terrorists because the problem is here and it will not go away. He also added that Canada accepted the reality of the dangers that extremists posed in October when a soldier was killed at the National War Memorial by a radicalized Canadian gunman before proceeding to the parliament building.

Benjamin Netanyahu sent a letter of condolence to Francois Hollande the Prime Minister of France which he later tweeted.

Shimon Peres, former president of Israel, attended a memorial gathering and expressed his condolences at the French Ambassador's home in Jaffa. Shimon Peres said that the people that died in the attack did so in the fight for freedom. He went on to say that in the end freedom will prevail and France will prevail.

The French Ambassador expressed his gratitude to the Israeli people for the solidarity they showed. He later went on to say that no act, no matter how horrifying, will be successful in cutting down freedom and that the French will also stand unified against terror, just like a wall.

The Search for the Gunmen Involved in the Attack

The two gunmen responsible for the attack were suspected to be brothers. The anti-terrorism police started conducting a search a day after the attack. The searches were done house to house in the north east villages of Paris.

The gunmen were believed to have been seen in ski masks in a petrol station a few kilometers from a village known as Corcy. Police officers were searching that area as well. The suspects robbed a service station found in the northern part of France. They stole both food and gas at the petrol station. French media disclosed information that the two suspected gunmen were indeed armed and had been spotted driving away in a white Renault Clio. Reports said they were wearing rain coats and masks and one could see their weapons which were at the back of the vehicle. In addition to a ground search, helicopters were also used in the search and could be seen flying overhead.

The Longonot Village, where searches were being conducted, is located about seventy kilometers from the northern part of Paris. It has a boggy marshland and thick forest but there was no confirmation regarding whether the attackers were hiding in the area or if they had moved to some other place.

The residents of Corcy had bewildered looks when they saw heavily armed policemen searching the village in helmets and ski masks. They combed the entire place from garages to barns to houses.

A Corcy villager named Jacques said that there were rumors that the fugitives could be in the forest, but nothing had been confirmed at that point so they were also watching the television to get any information that might be available.

A resident of the neighboring Longonot Village said the police had advised them to stay indoors during the search because there was a possibility that the gunmen's car was abandoned somewhere in the village and the suspects had fled into the woods on foot. The Anti-terrorism officers combed the area until dark.

Although the police were unable to find the suspects on that particular day, they did not rest. The government deployed more than eighty thousand police officers to help in the search. Investigators did not sleep but instead tried to learn as much as they could about the attackers.

Said Kouachi and Cherif were 34 and 32 years old, respectively. They were born on the eastern part of Paris, but their parents died and they had to grow up in an orphanage located in the city of Rennes.

The gunmen brothers were born in France though their parents were born in Algeria. They had already been placed under police surveillance at the time of the Paris attack. Cherif Kouachi had been arrested when attempting to travel to Iraq to join an Islamic fighting group. He was arrested in 2005 when he was planning to fly to Syria through Iraq to combat Americans and was sentenced to three years but only served eighteen months. Vincent Olliver, the lawyer who represented Cherif, told the Liberty Daily that he was not really a dangerous fanatic but just a lost and confused young man. This was a decade ago. They had been described as, "armed and dangerous" by the police. He had been quoted saying that he was ready to die in battle because he could not stand the injustices that he saw the Americans inflicting on the Iraqis on television.

He was suspected in 2010 as being a member of a group that had attempted to break Smain Ali Belkacem from prison. Smain Ali Belkacem was a militant found guilty of organizing and executing the bombings of metro and Paris stations in 1995 which subsequently left eight people dead and one-hundred and twenty wounded. A case against was opened Cherif Kouachi but was later dismissed on the grounds of lack of evidence.

The fact that the police had this kind of information raised some questions as to whether the police would have done more to prevent the attack or arrest the gunmen before they committed their heinous act.

Said Kouachi, who was one of the brothers, had trained with the Al Qaeda for some months in Yemen in 2011. He was said to be in AQAP in the Arabian Peninsula. This is believed to be one of Al Qaeda's most active affiliates.

Chérif **KOUACHI**
né le 29/11/1982

Said **KOUACHI**
né le 07/09/1980

A Yemeni official who had insights on the matter confirmed that the government of Yemen had been aware of a possible connection between Said Kouachi and the Al Qaeda group and that they were in the process of looking for possible links at the time of the attack.

Sources of the U.S government said that indeed the two brothers Cherif Kouachi and Said Kouachi were on the list of the U.S security databases. This highly classified database known as TIDE consists of information on many terrorist suspects. Approximately 1.2 million are on this list and it is maintained by an interagency unit known as the Terrorist Screening Center. According to ABC, which is a U.S television network, the brothers' names have been in the databases for several years.

When contacted, the Terrorist Screening Centre's spokesman, Dave Joly, neither confirmed nor denied the existence of the names of the two brothers on their databases.

The day following the Paris attack, the U.S President Barack Obama visited the French Embassy in Washington. His visit was unannounced and he said he was there to pay his respects. He even went ahead to write on the condolence book and these were his words, "As allies across the centuries, we stand united with our French brothers to ensure that justice is done and our way of life is defended. We go forward together knowing that terror is no match for freedom and ideals we stand for – ideas that light the world."

The Reaction of the French to the Attack

France had a tearful and perplexed nation on the national day of mourning for the people who died in the Charlie Hebdo attack, whose cartoons were recognized nationally.

World leaders sent their message of condolences and said the attack was an assault on democracy. The North Africa Al Qaeda's branch, on the other hand, had praises for the act and referred to the attackers as "knights of truth".

On the same day of the Charlie Hebdo attack, word was going around of revenge attacks to be carried out on Muslims in different parts of France. However, no one was injured or lost their life.

The local police detonated a makeshift explosive device outside a kebab near a mosque in eastern France. The local police however, did not make a direct connection to the Charlie Hebdo attack. A Muslim prayer hall found in southern France had two shots fired at it while other shots were fired at a parked car that belonged to a family whose origin was that of North African.

While on RTL radio, the Prime Minister was asked whether he had fears of other attacks taking place. His response was that security is the government's main concern and the reason many investigators and police are in place to ensure they catch the criminals.

The French authorities tightened security after the Charlie Hebdo attack and this was seen in media offices, at transport hubs, in stores and on religious sites. There was also increased police presence at Paris' entry points.

Several white police vans could be seen at Porte d'Orleans which is one of the main gateways of Paris. There were officers with rifles and bulletproof jackets. Two-hundred extra soldiers were provided by the defense protection to offer added security to Paris.

There were vigils held across France on January 7, 2015 when the Charlie Hebdos offices were attacked. People turned up in the thousands wearing badges and holding placards reading, "Je suis Charlie" to show their support for the freedom of speech that the news magazine was exercising.

There were moments of silence to honor the departed in different parts of France the day after the attack. The same thing happened in Brussels at the European Parliament. In addition to that, the Eiffel Tower lights were dimmed to show solidarity together with the Charlie Hebdo attack victims. The Israeli flag at the embassy in

Paris was flying at half-staff as a way of showing their solidarity and condolence with the people of France.

Millions of people marched both in Paris and around the world to show the world that they refuse to walk in fear. O this day, Jews, Christians and Muslims came together for the same cause. Different leaders from all over the world came out to support the people. It was different because the march was not in protest but to say that they will not let terrorists win.

There was a unit rally organized on Sunday 11th of January four days after the attack. The theme was celebrating the values behind by the great people of Charlie Hebdo who died in the attack. David Cameron, the British Prime Minister, traveled to Paris to attend the event.

After the attack, a columnist for the Charlie Hebdo news magazine, Patrick Pelloux, spoke to CNN and said that he was not sure if he was afraid anymore after what happened to his friends. "I don't know if I'm afraid anymore, because I've seen fear. I was scared for my friends, and they are dead." He went on to say that he knew the fellow staff members who were slain and they would not want them to be quiet.

Although the attack on Charlie Hebdo news magazine was meant to stop them from further publishing images of the prophet Muhammad and possibly have others learn from it, this was not the reaction that followed. Most of the European newspaper took the opportunity to re-publish those same cartoons that had angered the killers. In addition to that, they added some of their own images.

The Daily Telegraph of Britain published cartoons of two gunmen standing the building of Charlie Hebdo telling each other, "Be careful, they might have pens."

The Muslim organizations implored imams across the country to condemn terrorism by preaching this message during their Friday prayers. The imams of the different mosques were called to strongly condemn terrorism regardless of where it originates.

Muslims were also requested to be part of a dignified and silent gathering. After that, they were to honor the victims during the Friday prayers which were two days after the Charlie Hebdo attack. There are usually national commemorative events held in France which can also act as the platform for preaching peace and expression of their condolences for the victims of the Charlie Hebdo attack. Muslim organizations expressed their shock at the murder of their journalist. They said they were empathizing with the victims of the attack and the pain that the families of the victims were enduring. In general, the Muslim organizations just wanted to show their solidarity.

Richard Malka, Charlie Hebdo's lawyer, said that the news magazine would continue to publish their content and in fact, would increase the number of copies to a million which is more than the usual figure of sixty thousand normally printed. Google promised to give the publication one-quarter of a million pounds as a way of showing their support.

The shooting was condemned by Muslim leaders who expressed fears of anti-Islamic feeling in France due to the act even though the largest population is Muslims. Eric Holder, the U.S .Attorney

General, flew to Paris four days after the attack to discuss ways in which they can counter violent extremism.

The United States provided the French investigators with the help they needed to track down the gunmen who attacked the Charlie Hebdo building. This helped the French police to identify the gunmen as brothers with the names Said Kouachi and Cherif.

In the wake of the Charlie Hebdo attack, new policies were proposed in France. Another issue which was subject to discussion was the suggestion of sharing records of air passengers among the EU states. All of these policies were in an attempt to strengthen security in the country and bring the culprits to justice. The president of France, Francois Hollande, said the attack on the Charlie Hebdo news magazine happened in the capital city and it is like the country being struck at the heart.

Subsequent Attacks After the Charlie Hebdo Attack

On the 8th of January, 2015, a day after the attack at the Charlie Hebdo offices in Paris, a woman was shot by two men in the southern part of Paris and later succumbed to her injuries. A police officer by the name Clarisa Jean – Philippe, age 27, and a colleague were assaulted by two men who opened fire when they went to respond to a reported traffic accident case.

The police officer had only worked in that particular job for fifteen days. Other people who were at the crime scene with Clarissa included a colleague and a street cleaner. One gunman fled on foot, but the other was arrested at the crime scene. The street cleaner was shot while trying to disarm the gunman. He was rushed to the hospital in serious condition.

Shortly after the shooting, a convoy of counter-terrorism police was sent to the scene of the crime bearing heavy arms.

This further increased the already present tension among the citizens of France. Police were not able to say at the time, however, whether or not that particular incidence had any connection to the previous day's attack on the Charlie Hebdo news magazine. The authorities started another terrorism investigation based on that attack.

The French Interior Minister arrived at the scene of the incident and said there was no clear proof that the shooting was connected to the Charlie Hebdo attack. He asked the people to exercise calm and restraint. The police later confirmed that both suspects had been arrested and one of them was an older man, aged 52. The balaclava-clad officers were thirty in number and they arrived in an armored lorry and five vehicles. The police team later left after failing to get any trace of the gunman who fled.

The police union officials confirmed that the suspect had a semi-automatic rifle and a pistol. Emmanuel Cravello, representing the Alliance police union, gave a statement to the effect that the gunman stopped their vehicle on Avenue Pierre Brosdolette and started shooting which resulted in the policewoman receiving fatal wounds. He fled leaving his car two and a half miles from the crime scene. The vehicle left behind was a white Renault Clio which is the same type of car as the one that the Charlie Hebdo attackers were reported to have hijacked.

On eye witness said that the assailant had on a bullet –proof vest and was dressed in black while another witness was sure that one of them was African. This ruled out the possibility that he might been one of the two brothers responsible for the Charlie Hebdo attacks.

The Fate of the Paris Shooting Culprits

An eighteen year old man surrendered at Charleville- Mezieres Police Station located near the Belgium border on the day of the Charlie Hebdo attack. A legal source said the man was one a brother in law to one of the Kouachi brothers. His friends said on social media that he was in school when the attack took place.

Two days after the killing of twelve people at the Charlie Hebdo offices in Paris, a number of raids were carried out by the French police. This resulted in to the death of three terrorists. Two of them were suspected to be the gunmen behind the shooting at Charlie Hebdo while the third suspect was involved in a shooting which led to the death of a policewoman and four people being taken hostages. After their deaths, many hostages were freed.

The Interior Minister, Bernard Cazeneuve, gave a statement saying that although the work of the government is not yet over and they still have to find a woman who shot a woman who was involved in the shooting of a police woman, killing the three terrorists and freeing the hostages was a sign of relief for the nation.

The Paris Prosecutor, Francois Molin, told investigators that the wife of Cherif Kouachi and the girlfriend of Amedy Coulibaly (suspected of killing a policewoman) communicated five hundred times through phone calls in 2014. When Cherif's wife was contacted by investigators she confirmed that Coulibaly and Cherif were well acquainted with one another.

Cherif Kouachi was suspected to be one of the gunmen behind the Charlie Hebdo attack while Amedy Coulibaly was suspected of killing a policewoman together with a woman by the name Hayat Boumeddiene on the next day after the Charlie Hebdo attack. Hayat Boumeddiene (female in the next picture) on the other hand was still at large.

On the 9th of January, 2015, a shootout between the police and an armed terrorist near a kosher grocery store in Paris led to the death of four hostages with fifteen survivors. On that day, the Kouachi brothers went to a print shop located in an industrial area. A salesman known as Didier said that he shook the hands of one of the gunmen at about 8:30 am when they arrived at the shop. The witness said that he mistook the gunman for a police officer due to the way he was dressed up in black and was heavily armed. As they were leaving the man told him to go because they do not kill civilians which he thought was not normal but he did not have an idea of what was happening.

The area the gunmen were in was then locked down. Roads were closed, shops were shuttered and children were stuck in schools. The gunmen then said they wanted to be like martyrs in their death.

Gunshots were heard inside the shop a few minutes after 5 pm followed by at least three explosions which were so large that they pierced the silence. Some men were seen on the roof afterwards and for helicopters made their landing nearby.

There was word after that concerning the brothers being dead and a man who was hiding inside the building was safe.

The same incident happened at a kosher grocery store which is forty kilometers or twenty-five miles away from Porte de Vincennes in Paris, although the character was different. Here it was Amedy Coulibaly who took several hostages. The gunman, Amedy Coulibaly, then called BFMTV after taking the hostages and he had demands which he wanted met. According to witnesses at the scene, he demanded that the Kouachi brothers be given their freedom. There were dozens of law enforcement officials that flooded the area.

A few minutes afterwards there were explosions and gunfire. Heavily armed police officers were able to enter the store and retrieve a number of civilians. However, not everyone survived, four people lost their lives. According to Israeli government sources, President Hollande of France had a phone conversation with Benjamin Netanyahu the Prime Minister of Israel in which he told him that four hostages had died and fifteen were rescued.

When the man suspected to be Amedy Coulibaly called BFMTV, which is an affiliate of CNN, he confirmed that he was a member of the Islamist militant group ISIS and that he had been sent by al

Qaeda to carry out the massacre. He further went on to add that the late Anwar al-Awlaki was the one who financed his trip. CNN however, cannot confirm if the recording was authentic.

Al-Awlaki was a Muslim scholar born in America and later became al Qaeda's spokesperson in the Arabian Peninsula. He died by a CIA drone strike in 2011.

The same day of these two events, President Hollande gave a statement saying that the deaths that occurred that day were an, "anti-Semitic act". He urged the citizens of France not to retaliate on the Muslims with use of violence. "Unity is our weapon," he said.

The students that were locked in the school were able to leave while police officers accompanied them holding their hands and even lifting some of them on to a waiting bus ready to take them to safety.

A parent, who asked to be referred to as Teddy, was outside the school ready to pick up his five year old son when the events unfolded. He said he did not have the words to explain what happened to his son because it was like a war.

It was mentioned earlier that Cherif was arrested for being involved in the attempt to break an Algerian named Smain Ali Belkacem from prison in 2010 although the case was dismissed due to lack of evidence. It turned out that Coulibaly was his accomplice in the incident.

Coulibaly had a Kalashnikov rifle, two-hundred and forty rounds of ammunition and Djamel Beghal's photo with him when he was arrested. Djamel Beghal was a French Algerain who was famous for recruiting many Muslims from Europe in to al Qaeda. According to the western intelligence source, Coulibaly and Boumeddiene, his alleged accomplice, lived together.

The attack at the Charlie Hebdo news magazine happened when the staff was having their weekly meeting. A former Charlie Hebdo writer, Edouuard Perrin, said he was in an office across the hall when the shootings started and he took cover. He was one of the first people to enter the hall after the killers had left. He said that they met an absolute carnage when they got inside the hall. He said that there were both dead people and survivors. They started ministering CPR on the survivors to give them a better chance at fighting for their lives. Edouuard said he touched one person who was lying on the ground but did not get a pulse.

Forensic experts started looking for DNA or any clues as to who the attackers could have been. They looked on the streets and at the sealed offices too. The people who managed to capture the events of the attack on their cellphone posted the photos and videos online. Others went for the security –camera video in order to show the world the events that took place and to try and see if there was anything that could help in the hunt for the terrorists.

Other Terrorist Attacks in the Previous Years

France had been resilient in their fight against Islamic extremists in the previous years. The French military even joined the forces loyal to the government of Mali in order to try and push back on the attacks made by the Islamist militants. When the U.S made efforts to conduct bombing raids in Iraq and to thwart the efforts of the Islamic State in Syria, France was actually the first country to join them.

The previous weeks before the attack had the French people on edge. This is due to the fact that just before Christmas a man was shot after he stabbed three police officers in central France and then went about yelling, " God is great" in Arabic which translates to "Allahu akbar."

In addition to that, there were two separate incidences in both Dijon and Nantes where men drove vehicles into crowds killing a total of twenty-three people. When that happened, two hundred to three hundred military personnel were deployed on the streets to ensure more security even though there were already seven-hundred and eighty of them on the ground.

Prior to the Paris attacks during the week of the January 7th, 2015, there had been other terrorist attacks in the previous years both in France and Europe at large.

In 1995, a Paris subway train was bombed leaving at least twenty-nine people injured. Of the twenty-nine, five of them had very serious injuries where one person's legs were all amputated on the train.

Remains of a 3kg cooking gas were later found on the train. The cooking gas had explosives and screws to act as shrapnel. After the attack, Algerian Islamic extremists claimed responsibility for the blasts.

Their aim was to force France to stop helping Algerian military rulers in their fight against terrorism.

The train was moving at a speed of 60 kph (kilometers per hour), which is equivalent to 35 mph. It was going through a tunnel located between Orsay Museum Metro and Saint- Michel stations when the bomb exploded. According to the eyewitness accounts, the bomb exploded as the train was approaching the station. There was dense smoke underground which left many passengers dazed because they did not even know what was going on. There were several ambulances rushed to the scene and they were able to help many people.

Before this attack there were some bombs which were found earlier on. Police were successful in defusing two of them and one misfired. The bombs found in these cases were made using nails and bolts which was a technique common with the GIA in Algeria.

In 1985, a hotel in the suburban areas of Athens, Greece was bombed leaving twelve people injured and many guests at the hotel panicking and scrambling to flee to the streets.

A London hotel had four stories and had the ground floor destroyed by the explosion. A British tourist by the name of Michelle Corder was among those seriously injured. He was rushed to the hospital where, fortunately, his condition stabilized and the others were also released from hospital after treatment. Most of those injured had cuts from shattered glass and other objects.

Although police reports indicated that a gas leak was the cause of the explosion, someone who claimed to be one of the Muslim extremists groups known as "the Organization of Socialist revolution" called a French news agency to claim responsibility for the attack. He said that the attack targeted, "British groups that habitually frequent the hotel under the cover of tourism to make it a centre of espionage and to elaborate their aggressive plans against our Arab and Islamic regions."

A bartender by the name of Pericles Malamos said that most of the injured people were sitting around by the pool drinking night caps when the blast occurred. The bartender also had various cuts on his arms and legs.

Conclusion

The Paris shooting took many by surprise. However, after recovering, the French government found ways of dealing with the tragedy and putting measures in place that would prevent such terrorist acts in the future. As the world mourned with France, it served as a lesson to show that terrorism is real and it will not go away despite our wishes.

Several meetings were held with different state leaders who expressed their condolences and joined together in the fight against terrorism. Many governments learned from what happened to France and tried to do better in their own respective countries. Therefore the attack on Charlie Hebdo offices in Paris, due to the freedom of expression they were exercising, has shown leaders that the freedom of the press is quite important and should be respected.

The work that the people (particularly the cartoonists) lost their lives for has not died. There have been some small terrorist attacks but the Paris shooting had a higher level of sophistication and the gunmen involved showed a high level of training too. This means that terrorists are becoming more experienced and serious when it comes to following up on threats and not letting anyone stand in their way.

Different newspapers have taken up the war against terror in the hope that someday people would be able to live their lives peacefully without worrying about who will come out to attack them as they go about their daily lives.